Books by Edward Hirsch

THE NIGHT PARADE   1989

WILD GRATITUDE   1986

FOR THE SLEEPWALKERS   1981

The Night Parade

The Night Parade

For Kim —

in deep admiration

for your wonderfully gifted

poems

warm greetings, [signature]

POEMS BY

Edward Hirsch

ALFRED A. KNOPF   NEW YORK   2003

Grateful acknowledgment is made to the editors of the following publications where these poems first appeared:

The Agni Review: "Rapture"
The American Poetry Review: "Skywriting," "Cross Portrait" (under the title "Portrait of the Artist with John Egner")
The Atlantic: "Execution"
Boulevard: "Refusal"
The Gettysburg Review: "Siblings"
Grand Street: "Cemetery by the Sea: Ha'iku"
The Nation: "My Grandfather's Poems," "Evening Star," "In the Underground Garage"
The New England Review/Bread Loaf Quarterly: "My Father's Back"
The New Criterion: "American Apocalypse"
The New Republic: "Homage to O'Keeffe," "A Short Lexicon of Torture in the Eighties," "Birds of Paradise," "Infertility"
The New Yorker: "Memorandums," "My Grandmother's Bed," "Incandescence at Dusk"
The Ontario Review: "Family Stories"
The Quarterly: "And Who Will Look Upon Our Testimony"
The Reaper: "The Abortion (1969)"
Shenandoah: "For the New World"
Southwest Review: "Proustian"
The Western Humanities Review: "A Photograph Ripped in Half," "Cemetery by the Sea: Kahuku"
The Yale Review: "When Skyscrapers Were Invented in Chicago"

I wish to express my gratitude to the John Simon Guggenheim Foundation for a grant which allowed me to complete this book.

Special thanks to Michael Collier, Garrett Hongo, Richard Howard, Philip Levine, and Jim Shepard. My deepest thanks to Janet Landay for her encouragement and faith.

Library of Congress Cataloging-in-Publication Data

Hirsch, Edward.
    The night parade.
      I. Title.
PS3558.I64N5   1989   811'.54   88–45798
ISBN 0–394–57720–6
ISBN 0–679–72299–8 (pbk.)

Manufactured in the United States of America
Published April 17, 1989
Reprinted Five Times
Seventh Printing, November 2003

But he would have us remember most of all
To be enthusiastic over the night
    Not only for the sake of wonder
    It alone has to offer, but also

Because it needs our love. . . .

        W. H. Auden
        In Memory of Sigmund Freud

Contents

Memorandums   3

1

My Grandmother's Bed   7
My Grandfather's Poems   8
Evening Star   9
Homage to O'Keeffe   10
Incandescence at Dusk   12
Skywriting   14
A Short Lexicon of Torture in the Eighties   16
And Who Will Look Upon Our Testimony   18

2

Birds-of-Paradise   29
Siblings   31
My Father's Back   37
Execution   39
In the Underground Garage   41
For the New World   43
When Skyscrapers Were Invented in Chicago   45
American Apocalypse   48

3

Family Stories   55

CONTENTS

4

Rapture	69
Refusal	71
The Abortion (1969)	73
A Photograph Ripped in Half	75
Cemeteries by the Sea	77
Cross Portrait	81
Infertility	83
Proustian	84

The Night Parade

Memorandums

*"I feel anxious to insert these
memorandums of my affections. . . ."*
JOHN CLARE

I put down these memorandums of my affections
    To stave off the absolute,
  To stave off the flat palm of the wind
      Pressed against the forehead of night,
    To stave off the thought of stars
Swallowed by the constellations of darkness.

Winter descends in knives, in long sheets of ice
    Unravelling in the sky,
  In stuttering black syllables of rain.
      There's a vise grinding on my temples
    And the sound of a hammer thudding
Somewhere far back in my mind. I can't sleep,

And when I sleep I dream of murky chemicals
    Washing across the faces
  Of my grandparents floating face down
      In a swimming pool. I dream of un-
    Born children drifting overhead
And out of reach. I dream of blinding lights.

I put down these memorandums of my affections
    In honor of my mother
  And my mother's mother who cooled
      My forehead with a damp washcloth,
    My two sisters and the aunt
Who ministered to my headaches in childhood,

My grandfather who kissed me on the upper arm
And tucked me in
At night, my father who touched
The blanket in the morning, gently.
I think of my mother-in-law
And my friend—my only brother—who died

Because cancer feasted on their ripe bodies
From the inside.
I remember the ravaged stillness
And peacefulness of their faces,
Their open lips and sealed eyes
As they were zippered in bags and carted away.

I put down these memorandums of my affections
In honor of tenderness,
In honor of all those who have been
Conscripted into the brotherhood
Of loss, who have survived
The ice and the winter descending in knives.

We will be lifted up and carried a far distance
On invisible wings
And then set down in an empty field.
We will carry our hearts in our bodies
Over shadowy tunnels and bridges.
Someday we will let them go again, like kites.

1

My Grandmother's Bed

How she pulled it out of the wall
To my amazement. How it rattled and
Creaked, how it sagged in the middle
And smelled like a used-clothing store.
I was ecstatic to be sleeping on wheels!

It rolled when I moved; it trembled
When she climbed under the covers
In her flannel nightgown, kissing me
Softly on the head, turning her back.
Soon I could hear her snoring next to me—

Her clogged breath roaring in my ears,
Filling her tiny apartment like the ocean
Until I, too, finally swayed and slept
While a radiator hissed in the corner
And traffic droned on Lawrence Avenue. . . .

I woke up to the color of light pouring
Through the windows, the odor of soup
Simmering in the kitchen, my grandmother's
Face. It felt good to be ashore again
After sleeping on rocky, unfamiliar waves.

I loved to help her straighten the sheets
And lift the Murphy back into the wall.
It was like putting the night away
When we closed the wooden doors again
And her bed disappeared without a trace.

My Grandfather's Poems

I remember that he wrote them backwards,
In Yiddish, in tiny, slanting, bird-like lines
That seemed to rise and climb off the page
In a flurry of winged letters, mysterious signs.

Scrupulously he copied them out
On the inside covers of his favorite books
While my sister and I romped through the house
Acting like cops and robbers, cowboys and crooks,

Whooping, shouting, and gunning each other down
In the hallway between rooms, mimicking fright,
Staggering from wall to bloody wall before
Collapsing in wild giggles at his feet.

Always he managed to quiet us again,
Kissing us each on the upper part of the arm,
Tucking us in. . . . We never said prayers,
But later I could hear him in the next room

Talking to himself in a low, tearing whisper—
All I could fathom was a haunted sound
Like a rushing of waves in the distance,
Or the whoosh of treetops in the back yard.

For years I fell asleep to the rhythm
Of my grandfather's voice rising and falling,
Filling my head with his lost, unhappy poems:
Those faint wingbeats, that hushed singing.

Evening Star

(Georgia O'Keeffe in Canyon, Texas, 1917)

She was just a schoolteacher then
Walking away from the town
                  in the late-afternoon sunset,
A young woman in love
                with a treeless place,
The scattered windmills and pounding winds
Of the whole prairie sliding toward dusk,
Something unfenced and wild
                  about the world without roads,
Miles and miles of land
                rolling like waves into nowhere,
The light settling down in the open country.

She had nothing to do but walk away
From the churches and banks, the college buildings
Of knowledge, the filling stations
                  of the habitable world,
And then she was alone
                with what she believed—
The shuddering iridescence of heat lightning,
Cattle moving like black lace in the distance,
Wildflowers growing out of bleached skulls,
The searing oranges and yellows of the evening star
Rising in daylight,
                  commanding the empty spaces.

Homage to O'Keeffe

That year I lived with a colorful print
Of her *Evening Star* nailed to the wall
Of my dark cell
                  above Jackson's Bridal Shop,
Its one grimy window
                        facing the autograph tree
In front of the bus station across the street.

Each morning I'd wake up to the voice
Of a disc jockey blaring above the gears
Of the #23 bus
                  starting its rounds for the day;
Each night I'd lie down to the music
Of buses returning,
                    the janitor's saw in the basement.

It hurts me to remember how I lived then,
Desolate as my narrow room, roaming the streets
Hour after hour
                  as if I were carrying out the terms
Of a life-sentence,
                    condemned to search
The blank, exhausted faces of passing strangers. . . .

Only the evening star soothed me.
I'd lie on my cot imagining
                    the low, mournful, flute-like voices
Of cattle moving across the prairie
                      in slow motion
Under the cumulus white clouds
                    rolling over the earth.

I loved the bright intensity of fire
In the darkening sky,
                the way it hung suspended
In blue-black space—
                calm, searing, apart—
Surviving the nightfall,
                enduring the emptiness.

Incandescence at Dusk

(Homage to Dionysius the Areopagite)

There is fire in everything,
                      shining and hidden—
Or so the saint believed. And I believe the saint:
Nothing stays the same
                      in the shimmering heat
Of dusk during Indian summer in the country.

Out here it is possible to perceive
That those brilliant red welts
                      slashed into the horizon
Are like a drunken whip
                      whistling across a horse's back,
And that round ball flaring in the trees
Is like a coal sizzling
                      in the mouth of a desert prophet.

Be careful.
Someone has called the orange leaves
                      sweeping off the branches
The colorful palmprints of God
                      brushing against our faces.
Someone has called the banked piles
                      of twigs and twisted veins
The handprints of the underworld
Gathering at our ankles and burning
                      through the soles of our feet.
We have to bear the sunset deep inside us.

I don't believe in ultimate things.
I don't believe in the inextinguishable light
                                    of the other world.
I don't believe that we will be lifted up
                            and transfixed by radiance.
One incandescent dusky world is all there is.

But I like this vigilant saint
Who stood by the river at nightfall
And saw the angels descending
                            as burnished mirrors and fiery wheels,
As living creatures of fire,
                    as streams of white flame. . . .

1500 years in his wake,
I can almost imagine
                    his disappointment and joy
When the first cool wind
                    starts to rise on the prairie,
When the soothing blue rain begins
                            to fall out of the cerulean night.

Skywriting

(Harper Grace Hospital, July 15, 1984)

Through the west window
                    I could see a fractured moon
Installed in the smokestacks behind the house,
Almost full, frail in the half-rain, half-mist
Of a midsummer twilight
                    that lingered for a long time
On the slanted roofs
               and died on the black top of the river.

All afternoon my friend slept—
                    his breathing labored, dogged, intense—
As the colors seeped visibly
                out of the air-conditioned air
(A steady sifting of purples and blues,
                    bloodless oranges and pinks)
While darkness thickened on the white walls
And shadows crept like a judgment across the floor.

It's hard to bring back
               the slow terror of that afternoon
In a sterile place, my friend's dream
Of health drifting further and further away
From his body,
            almost palpable in the cool air,
A cloud above his head,
              the breath stuttering in his lungs. . . .

For me, it was like being called to the window
To see our two bodies in the rainy light
               of a darkness falling,

The faint, bluish-white twins
                    of Gemini rising
And splitting apart,
                    a barge pulling a single star
Over the swollen, accidental faces of trees.

That night I saw living and dying in everything,
Even in long bands of light
                    climbing out of the water,
One rainbow penetrating the night sky
While a second one arched
                    over its spectral head,
The bodies luminous and doubled,
                    their colors reversed.

A Short Lexicon of Torture in the Eighties

That's not a man in pain
                    but *a Brazilian phone*—
It won't be making any outgoing calls.

That's not a woman sprawling on the floor
But *an old-fashioned dance,*
                    like the tango.

Pull up a chair with a knotted rope.
Let's have *a tea party with toast*
                    and *hors d'oeuvres.*

Let's take a seat
                on *the parrot's perch.*
Let's rock to *the motorola* with headphones.

Do you want to bathe
                in the porcelain tub?
Do you want to sing to *the little hare?*

Let's stroll over to *the guest room.*
Let's take a bus ride
                to *the San Juanica bridge.*

Forget the ovens and smokestacks.
Forge *the rack and screw,*
                the tiger's cage.

We're celebrating *a birthday party*
                           in your honor.
We're lighting candles on your favorite cake.

We're taking you to *a parade*
                           on a sandy beach.
You're going down in *a submarine.*

And Who Will Look Upon Our Testimony

On an unsuspecting Wednesday in October, 1347,
    A Genoese crew
  "Who had sickness clinging to their very bones"
    Brought the black rats and fleas
Flooding into the Messina harbor
        On the Northeast coast of Sicily.

The twelve galleys that landed had been driven
    By fierce winds
  From the East, infected and laden with spices.
    In three days the known world
Was changed forever by children
        Vomiting blood and howling for light.

It was changed by young Sicilian fishermen
    Who ran through town
  Screaming about the boils swelling in their
    Groins and under their armpits
Like blistering almonds,
        Like rotting eggs or apples.

The brackish blotches seethed and spread,
    Oozing blood and pus
  Until they turned into fiery purple knobs
    And peas sprouting on the arms,
Brittle black sea coals
        And cinders burning under the skin,

So that the stricken began to shiver and dance
      In strange bodily fits.
   Soon people were falling down in convulsions,
      Whirling through the streets
In a grim trance, and dying
      In the terrible ecstasy of fever.

A mother saw the face of death seated on the face
      Of her startled daughter,
   A father saw the emeralds of death glowing
      In his son's eyes. The doctors believed
That one coughing child
      Could infect the world's bloodstream,

And within months the continent was so bewildered
      And stupefied by pain
   That fathers abandoned their children, and wives
      Escaped from their husbands, brothers
Turned away from their sisters,
      And mothers denied their sons.

Peasants fled from their cramped hamlets and towns,
      Leaving the wheat uncut
   And the harvest untended, the sheep roaming
      Aimlessly through the countryside
Until they, too, collapsed and
      Died in the ditches and hedgerows.

Some people imagined a black giant striding
      Across the land,
   Others saw the Fourth Horseman of the Apocalypse.
      Some believed the plague had descended
In a rain of serpents and scorpions
      When sheets of fire fell on the earth.

There were misty clouds, hot winds from the South.
        A column of fire
    Twisted above the papal palace of Avignon,
        And in Venice the tremoring earth
Set the bells of St. Mark's pealing
          Without being touched by calloused hands.

The dancing went on. There were places where
        "No one was left
    To bury the dead, for money or friendship,
        And whole villages scattered, like dust
To the wind." No one mourned,
          Nor did the death bells toll.

"In Siena great pits were dug and piled deep
        With the multitude of dead.
    And they died by the hundreds, nay, thousands,
        Both day and night, night and day,
And all were thrown into ditches
          And covered up with the earth.

The people said and believed, *This is the end*
        Of the world!
    Blessed are those who did not witness
        The horror." Blessed are those
Who never fell victim to
          The dancing mania and the stupor.

The Welsh sang of death coming into their midst
        Like black smoke,
    Like a rootless phantom who cuts down the young
        And shows no mercy to the fair.
Woe is me of the shilling
        And the black pest in the armpit!

A clergyman recorded the death of five thousand sheep
   In one field alone,
 "Their bodies so corrupted from the plague
   That neither beast nor bird
Would touch them." Preying wolves
    Fled to the safety of the wilderness.

Some danced to the sound of drums and trumpets
   Fighting the ghost
With the high jollity of a happy music.
   Some kept carefully unto themselves,
Barricaded into their homes,
    Avoiding the grasp of the Evil One.

The Pistoian merchants decided the Dance of Death
   Was a warning from Heaven
 About crooked businessmen from Pisa and Lucca,
   The Circassian slaves thought the spots
Growing on their hands and necks
    Were a punishment from their masters.

And in the country the peasants died grotesquely
   On the roads
 And in the fields. In the cities, the rich
   Fled and the poor died in burrows.
"And everywhere men and women
    Wandered around as if mad."

The people believed that the boils were God's
   Tokens and stamps.
 In April, some friars saw the Star of Pestilence
   Exploding in the sky after Vespers;
In May, some nuns saw the Angel
    Of Death rising over the steeples.

And still the corpses kept piling up in the streets
And the stench was foul.
In Paris, five hundred bodies a day were carried
In a procession of open carts
From the Hotel Dieu
To the cemetery of the Holy Innocents.

"And in these days was burying without sorrowe and
Wedding without friendschippe."
Priests bolted themselves inside of churches
And died alone. And penitents in sackcloths
Wound through the streets
Imploring the mercy of the Virgin

And hoping to appease Divine Wrath by sprinkling
Themselves with ashes,
By carrying candles and relics to the churches,
By tying ropes around their necks
And tearing out their hair
In acceptance of chastisement from Heaven.

The flagellants believed that God was punishing
The world for its sins,
And they roamed from town to town chanting
Hymns and wearing cowled white robes
Emblazoned with red crosses.
Some carried iron crosses in penance.

The martyrs gathered in a thick human circle
In the town square;
They stripped and scourged their naked torsos
With leather whips tipped with spikes
While the townsmen followed,
Groaning and sobbing in sympathy

And crazed women smeared the blood on their faces.
Across Central Europe
They were greeted as the frenzied redeemers
Of Christ the Tiger, Christ
The Avenging Angel, who rose up
And put his sword on their shoulders.

Soon they were rushing for the Jewish quarters,
Trailed by citizens
Howling for revenge and shrieking for blood.
And thus began the lynchings
And the slaughter of innocents
For poisoning wells and corrupting air.

Who will hear the testimony of eleven Savoy Jews
Who were burned alive
For carrying poison in narrow leather bags?
Who will hear the cries of the Basel Jews
Who were burned in wooden houses
That were built on an island in the Rhine?

At Speyer, the bodies of the murdered were piled
In great wine casks
And then sent cascading down the river.
On February 14, 1349, two thousand
Jews of Strasbourg were burned
In staked rows in the burial ground.

The four hundred Jews of Worms preferred to set
Themselves on fire.
And the Jews of Narbonne and Carcassonne
Were dragged out of their homes
And thrown into the flames.
No one listened to their cries.

"God is deaf now-a-days and deigneth not hear us."
The chronicler said,
"Things which should be remembered forever
Perish with time and vanish
From the memory
Of those who come after us."

The flagellants too dispersed, like night phantoms.
And now no one believes
That death is a black dog with a sword in its paws
Or that pestilence darts from the eyes
Or that a Pest Maiden emerges
From the lips in a clear blue flame

And flies from victim to victim. No one lights
Smoke pots against her visit,
Or falls down in terror before the wrathful God
Of the leper and the bloated sheep,
The corrupted bodies lying
In state for the starving dogs.

No one sings for the men and women who wandered
The world in madness
Or for the ghostly ships with their dead crews
Or for the chronicler who died
In the middle of an un-
Finished sentence about the plague:

"In the midst of this pestilence, there came
To an end. . . ."
Fortunate are those who come afterward,
The unfallen inheritors of earth
Who turn away from the Dance
Of Death dying in the mind.

"Oh happy posterity who will not experience
Such abysmal woe—
And who will look upon our testimony
As fable." Oh happy posterity
Who will die in its own time
With its own wondering tales of woe.

2

Birds-of-Paradise

Seven years after her death
I saw them again today, my mother-in-law's
Favorite flowers, a pair of streaked innocents,
Two large-blossomed angelic birds-of-paradise
Floating in a shop window on Second Avenue.

They looked stunned and unhappy, fragile
Long-stemmed bodies exiled behind a thicket
Of lilacs and daffodils, flowering azaleas
And a row of crimson roses flushed with color.
We were not meant to live in paradise.

But I remember so much about her last morning:
How we talked in her bedroom at five a.m.,
How the sun kissed the forehead of the house
And we fell asleep in adjacent white beds
With daylight streaming through the treetops.

Slowly the light curved along the ceiling,
Angled over the bookshelves, and drifted
Over the heads of two iridescent flowers
Propped in a glass bowl on the dresser.
Somewhere that light is still inside me

Shading the furniture, kindling the walls,
Crossing a bedroom with the dim purpose
Of settling into the mirror's long body. . . .
I stood on the sidewalk for a long time
Today staring into a flower shop window,

Remembering a silver body of sunlight
That reflected the outline of a man
And a woman lying together peacefully
With their faces tilted towards each other,
Their breath rising, their fingers intertwined.

Siblings

1

That small southpaw rocking forward on the mound
And scowling at a right-handed batter coiled in the box
In front of a stubby catcher calling for the pitch

Is my sister Lenie trying out for Little League
On a mild Sunday afternoon in mid-July, 1959.
I remember the triumph and exaltation

Of her blistering fastball rising at the knees
And her curveball nicking the corners at the waist
And her high off-speed changeup at the letters

That sent a string of cocky twelve-year olds
Back to the dugout shaking their heads in wonder
At a girl piling up strikeouts against them.

But my sister only remembers the humiliation
Of striking out so many older boys in a row
While their fathers gathered on the infield grass

And tried to persuade my stubbornly determined dad
That using a girl on the mound was against the rules,
All the while marveling at her masterful control.

The men in our family were proud of my sister's
Precocious slider and sloping curveball,
Her slow windup and sneaky whip-like quickness,

The way she mixed up her stuff and concentrated
On the target stationed on the outside corner,
Reaching inside herself for her best pitches.

But it wasn't until I listened to Lenie
Telling the story to a cousin twenty years later
At a Sunday afternoon picnic in Ravinia Park

That I understood how much she hated the memory
Of toeing the rubber and reducing so many older boys
To silence, their bats waving uselessly in the air. . . .

The story of siblings is the story of childhood
Experienced separately and together, one tree
Twisting in different directions, roots and branches,

One piece of land divided up into parcels,
Acres and half-acres, parts of a subdivision,
Memories carved into official and unofficial versions.

2

Some siblings are like bumper-cars
Banging each other a little too earnestly
At the amusement park on Saturday night,

Others are those small rivalries jostling
At a slumber party in a new classmate's house.
But mostly they are simultaneities sharing

A father and mother, different shapes moving
At different speeds in different directions
Through the same territory, one sister

Rushing up the stairs after an argument
While her brother races down them for a ballgame
And her younger sister plays in the sandbox.

These examples multiply into histories.
The night that Lenie was rushed to the hospital
With the first strange symptoms of neuralgia

(She was about to be put to bed for a year)
Was also the night that I was forced to wear
Girls pajamas and sleep on my aunt's bumpy sofa,

The night that I kissed Marcia on the mouth
In Lincolnwood Park while the legion band
Hammered out "Wild Thing" and "A Hard Day's Night"

Was also the night that Lenie highlighted
Her hair with blond streaks at Elaine's house
While Nancy was at home with the babysitter.

The three of us are standing next to each other
In family photographs, little descending heights
About to be herded into the car for vacation,

Or posing in front of the house for one major
Graduation or the other, one birthday or the next,
Our cousin Bernie's wedding, Aunt Lil's retirement.

The three of us are standing at the graveside
Of an uncle that everyone in the family adored
With an aunt who could be our older sister.

It's as if there's an invisible rope
Looped around our waists and holding us together
As we stare down into the same gaping hole.

3

And what about those sweet moments of harmony
Driving home from Lake Geneva, the three of us
Sleeping in the back seat in a tangle of limbs?

We are jumping all over our Uncle Robert
At a barbecue in our suburban back yard,
Trying to pin him down in the fresh sod

While our cousins Mickey, Allan, and Barbie
Are wrestling with their Uncle Kurt
On the other side of the badminton net.

Lenie and I are burying Nancy in sand
At the Morris Avenue beach, Nancy and I
Are splashing Lenie in the neighborhood pool,

Nancy and Lenie are taking turns riding
On the handlebars of my J. C. Higgins bicycle,
They are standing in the living-room in silence

While my father unbuckles his leather belt
For a little session with me in the basement
Because the principal had phoned him at work.

There was the afternoon that Nancy murdered me
At tennis for the first time while Lenie
Blasted my mother on the next court

And my father played golf with my Uncle Harry.
At sixty-five Harry is still the kid in the family
Trying to out-drive his older brother on the fairway.

We tell these stories to therapists and friends,
To strangers at parties who smile and nod
In recognition, remembering their own families

And the tales that get told to children
On holidays, the versions which get repeated
And the ones that are revealed later.

My sister Lenie is crossing the grass in spikes
While my teammates are elbowing me in the ribs
And my father is holding a baby in his arms,

Telling a story to the fathers and coaches,
To the manager who is glancing off at my mother
Taking a photograph of us from the stands.

My Father's Back

There's an early memory that I carry around
In my mind
        like an old photograph in my wallet,
A little graying and faded, a picture
That I don't much like
        but nonetheless keep,
Fingering it now and then like a sore tooth,
Knowing it's there,
        not needing to see it anymore. . . .

The sun slants down on the shingled roof.
The wind breathes in the needled pines.
And I am lying in the grass on my third birthday,
Red-faced and watchful
        but not squalling yet,
Not yet rashed or hived up
        from eating the wrong food
Or touching the wrong plant,
        my father's leaving.

A moment before he was holding me up
Like a new trophy, and I was a toddler
With my face in the clouds,
        spinning around
With a head full of stars,
        getting so dizzy.
A moment before I was squealing with joy
In the tilt-a-whirl of his arms,
Drifting asleep in the cavern of his chest. . . .

I remember waking up to the twin peaks
Of his shoulders moving away, a shirt clinging
To his massive body,
                a mountain receding.
I remember the giant distance between us:
A drop or two of rain, a sheen on the lawn,
And then I was sitting up
                in the grainy half-light
Of a man walking away from his family.

I don't know why we go over the old hurts
Again and again in our minds, the false starts
And true beginnings
                of a world we call the past,
As if it could tell us who we are now,
Or were, or might have been. . . .
                  It's drizzling.
A car door slams, just once, and he's gone.
Tiny pools of water glisten on the street.

Execution

The last time I saw my high school football coach
He had cancer stenciled into his face
Like pencil marks from the sun, like intricate
Drawings on the chalkboard, small *x's* and *o's*
That he copied down in a neat numerical hand
Before practice in the morning. By day's end
The board was a spiderweb of options and counters,
Blasts and sweeps, a constellation of players
Shining under his favorite word, *Execution*,
Underlined in the upper right-hand corner of things.
He believed in football like a new religion
And had perfect, unquestioning faith in the fundamentals
Of blocking and tackling, the idea of warfare
Without suffering or death, the concept of teammates
Moving in harmony like the planets—and yet
Our awkward adolescent bodies were always canceling
The flawless beauty of Saturday afternoons in September,
Falling away from the particular grace of autumn,
The clear weather, the ideal game he imagined.
And so he drove us through punishing drills
On weekday afternoons, and doubled our practice time,
And challenged us to hammer him with forearms,
And devised elaborate, last-second plays—a flea-
Flicker, a triple reverse—to save us from defeat.
Almost always they worked. He despised losing
And loved winning more than his own body, maybe even
More than himself. But the last time I saw him
He looked wobbly and stunned by illness,
And I remembered the game in my senior year
When we met a downstate team who loved hitting

More than we did, who battered us all afternoon
With a vengeance, who destroyed us with timing
And power, with deadly, impersonal authority,
Machine-like fury, perfect execution.

In the Underground Garage

I pulled my mother's baby-blue Thunderbird
Into a parking garage on the corner of Michigan and Lake
On a late afternoon in mid-December, one
Of those slushy Chicago dusks
When the air thickens around the Christmas lights
Strung through the evergreens that line the sidewalks,
And the diligent rush-hour traffic creeps along the lakeside
As if in obedience to a secret commandment,
And the shoppers sift through the fog.
The car hummed on the downward-spiraling ramp
And glided to a halt in front of a booth
Where a familiar-looking attendant in uniform—
I didn't recognize him at first—
Threw open a steel door and became
My closest friend from high school
Turning away in embarrassment. In a moment
We were in each other's arms,
But he wouldn't say a word
And already the cars were piling up behind us,
A row of impatience. He held the keys
To my mother's car and shifted his weight
Back on his heels—half in anger, half in disappointment—
As I saw him do on the sidelines against Maine South,
A linebacker's helmet imprinted on my back.
For an instant, I can see us
Putting our heads together in Jake's Diner
Over the memory of kisses from Marcia and Betty-Anne,
Or driving into Niles Township
For a beer-run in his father's pea-green Nova.
We were working side by side

In the old factory buried below Monroe Street,
Taking orders from the foreman on the second floor
And stacking cartons on top of cartons
On top of heavy wooden skids. . . .
But he didn't want to remember the past
Before our futures divided, before
Whatever was going to happen between us
Had already happened. The honking began
In earnest and the cars formed
A snake-like line curving up to the street,
Like souls in purgatory.
I thought of his father's labor
On the corrugator and the printing press, the years
His mother worked the night shift at Billings Container.
But before I could ask about them,
My friend slammed the door and screeched away
In the glistening blue car of privilege.
In silence he left me
Staring after him through the fog
And steam rising from the grated vents
At the buttresses and concrete dividers,
The spaces misting between us, the cars
Rolling into the underground depths at nightfall,
Filled with ghosts and strangers.

For the New World

(Auditorium Building, Chicago, Adler and Sullivan, 1887–1889)

The first idea was man walking through space in a tower
Of solid masonry carried on a floating foundation,
A raft weighing thirty million pounds and loaded down
With pig-iron and bricks, masses of timber and steel
Rails, three layers of I-beams. Think of it
As a farm boy planting his feet in the loose mud
And hoisting a city kid on his shoulders, a tower

Soaring on a strong Midwestern back, Adler and Sullivan's
Symphony in brick for the New World. Think of standing
At dawn on the recessed balcony above the Second City
For the first time, swaying in the wind and staring out
At the horizon-line where the lake meets the sky
On the edge of the prairie, something large and possible
In the long expanse of water and land, something blue

And plaintive in the brightening rhythms of morning,
A city to be built, the sun sweeping upwards. . . .
There is something American in the moment, something
Dark and innocent about our faith in a future rising
On the prairie, immense and open-hearted, the skeleton
Construction of skyscrapers just around the corner—
The old Schiller Building and the new Stock Exchange—

The idea of a "Garden City" growing out of rubble, the fire
That made the skyline possible, all the untimely mistakes
Swept away with the flames, the jerry-built houses and stores,
"The monstrous libels on artistic building," the past
Cancelled and destroyed at last, the country making way
For fireproof commercial buildings anchored in mud.
Who couldn't admire the strength of the underlying steel

Frame, the bones that carried tall buildings into heaven,
The idea that form followed function in a shell of offices
Surrounding a hotel with an L-shaped honeycomb of rooms
And a theater with elliptical arched trusses and perfect
Acoustics, a stage supported on a laminated floor?
On the gala opening night, the Apollo Club sang
A cantata composed by Frederick Grant Gleason,

And the prima donna, Adelina Patti, sang "Home Sweet Home"
To five-thousand cheering citizens. The future
Was still a possibility then—innocent, limitless, free—
And a city was about to be raised into the empty sky.
Think of it: the second idea was a tall office building
Artistically considered at the end of the Nineteenth Century.
The first idea was man walking through space in a tower.

When Skyscrapers Were Invented in Chicago

I think of it as a large moment with shadows
Expanding like a summer afternoon at the lake, sunspots

Blinking on the waves and a sudden burst of sails
Shivering in the distance like a mirage, the white clouds

Billowing with heat and floating over the water for miles,
The sky an emptiness to be scribbled across and filled.

It couldn't have happened without a democratic vision
Of time, the present finally equal to the past,

"Progress before precedent," as Louis Sullivan put it,
The self-evident proclamation of a city to be built

Into the sky, the need for fireproof buildings
And rentable space, a giant who could stand for years

With his feet in the mud and his head in the clouds
Withstanding the heat of mid-July and the icy winds

That blast off the lake in late December. To be sure,
It took a couple of hundred businessmen with American

Dreams of profit and plenty of credit, visionary
Architects and engineers who wanted to get rich

And were thrilled by the ugliness and dirt, the devastation
Of a fire that had started in a barn on DeKoven Street

And flamed across the river to the lake, turning north
And destroying everything in its path, whole neighborhoods

Flaring up like tinder, a city flattened
And reduced to rubble in a few days. After that,

It was an architect reaching upward with one arm
And sweeping away the past with the other,

Waving away the Federal Style and the Greek Revival,
Baroque east-coast imitations of the Romanesque.

It was a soaring moment with shadows, the steely
Gray shadows of the First and Second Leiter Buildings,

The Second Rand McNally and the Great Northern Hotel,
The Tacoma and the Cable, the Third McVickers Theater

And the original Stock Exchange. In the optimism
Of a moment of hydraulic elevators and complete

Iron framing (skeleton construction), the democratic
Revision of the pier, the lintel, and the arch,

Who could have imagined that most of these buildings
Would be demolished to make way for newer, taller skyscrapers?

Who would have believed that the streamlined future
Was about to be mortgaged and turned back into the past

At the beginning of a new century, in the competition
For the Tribune Building, the return to Gothic

After the World's Fair and the long Classical Revival
That destroyed Sullivan's career, New World architects

Crossing the ocean on steamers, pledging allegiance to Europe,
Even as houses, American houses, were growing on the prairie.

American Apocalypse

(Chicago, 1871)

It was as if God had taken a pen of fire
Into his flaming blue hand
And scrawled a chapter of horrors
Across the city at night,
Burning the world in a day-and-a-half. . . .

It was as if, after 98 days of drought,
The furious oranges and reds
Of the Last Judgment erupted
In a barn on DeKoven Street:
God had burnished the Gem on the Prairie.

Fire seethed through the shams and shingles,
Through the parched bodies
Of cottages and sheds, of cow-stables,
Corn-cribs, and pigsties,
All the tinder-dry precincts of Garden City.

The raised sidewalks were piles of kindling-
Sticks under pine and hemlock
Fences, the shanties were logs
Lit by kerosene. The barns
Were giant ovens exploding in a lumbermill.

The heavens blazed and a husky southern wind
Turned into a mass of devils
Whirling through the streets,
Advancing in a column
Of smoke and a wall of flame, a steady torrent

Of sparks and a shuddering wave of lightning
    Crackling in the air.
      The fire bells clanged and the
           Steamers stood by helplessly.
Soon the fire swept across the sluggish river

That flared like gasoline and seemed to boil
    In the 3,000 degree heat.
      It burned on three sides of the water
           At once, eating bridges and ships,
The huge grain elevators stacked along the banks.

First, the Tar Works exploded and then came
    The Gas Works and the Armory,
      The police station and the fire house,
           Conley's Patch. There were
Explosions of oil, crashes of falling buildings,

And down came the Post Office and the Water Works,
    The impregnable Board of Trade,
      The Opera House and the Design Academy,
           The sturdy Chamber of Commerce.
Down came the banks, the hotels, the churches. . . .

The tornado of fire rolled toward the north
    And people jammed the streets
      With wagons and carts, with
           Wheelbarrows of belongings.
They came tumbling out of windows and doorways,

Shrieking in all directions. There were horses
    Breathing smoke in dead alleys
And dogs racing like live torches
        Toward the burning water.
The noise was calamitous, torrential, deafening,

As the world staggered to a last fiery end.
    The firemen might as well
Have tried to arrest the wind itself
        Since the wind and the fire
Were a single fury hurtling through the night.

The dogs of Hell bounded over the rooftops
    And leaped from tree to tree.
There were no stars and no clouds,
        There was nothing else
In the sky but the fierce vengeance of flames

Flattening the world into stones and ashes.
    This was the Great Catastrophe
And some responded to the terror
        By kneeling down in embers
And crying out for release from the prophecy:

For behold, the Lord will come in fire and
    His chariots like the stormwind
To render his anger in fury
        And his rebuke with flames.
For by fire will the Lord execute judgment....

But then the judgment was stayed, the rains
Descended like manna,
Like a fresh pardon from Heaven,
And the winds calmed.
The fire devils died in the arms of the lake

And the wrath abated along the open ground
At the edge of Lincoln Park.
The Great Destruction was over
For the city in ruins.
So this was the smouldering end of Time.

And this was the Lightning City after 36 hours—
A muddy black settlement
On the plains, a ditched fort
After a quick massacre.
This was the Garden of Eden reduced into cinders.

The boom town had become an outpost again.
Soon the army was called in
To save the city from citizens
Who plundered and looted,
And stormed through the rubble in despair.

There were those who set themselves on fire,
Those who fled together
On the first trains heading east,
Those who cursed and wept
For the lost civilization on the prairie.

But there were also the unrepentant ones
Who were young and free
Of history at last. They moved
Through the ruins alone
In a jubilant new world blazing under the sun.

They stood in the cooling ashes without grief
And imagined their future
Rising out of the blue lake as
A man-made mountain range,
A city that aspired upward toward the sky.

3

Family Stories

I

I've been told about it so often
I feel as if I can actually remember
How much my grandfather hated the confusion

Of Maxwell Street on Sunday mornings in summer,
The crescendo of accents rising over the pushcarts
And stalls, the wagons of high-piled vegetables,

Buckets of used umbrellas and children's shoes,
Boxes of fresh underwear and discount shirts, block
After block of bargains on men's jackets and suits,

Shop windows festooned with colorful dresses.
I never visited the store on Fourteenth and Halsted
Where he worked the last eight years of his life

(I was eight when he died), but I heard often
About the voluble arguments that made him wince
Between his boss and the Spanish-speaking customers,

And the tiny refuge in the back where he kept
A photograph of his wife and daughters squinting
Into the sun on Independence Day in Grant Park.

I remember how much my mother and my aunt
Hated it for him, the long, killing hours,
Years of struggling for something extra,

The promise of dental school abandoned long ago
Like the study of Latin, the perfect Greek pronunciation,
The classical education wasted, or mostly wasted. . . .

And for what? Rye bread and galoshes. A couple
Of rooms off Logan Square. The red bicycle
My mother learned to ride in a single afternoon,

My aunt's first pair of earrings. These stories
Came down to us like the meat we ate as children
(Soft and overcooked, cut into squares)—

My grandfather dropping a suitcase of presents
On the wet stairs of the La Salle Street station,
The annual two-week vacation to Rochester, New York,

Aunt Celia's scrambled eggs, Uncle Max's impulsiveness—
The time he drove to Niagara Falls at midnight
With my grandparents asleep in the front seat

And five children scrunched up in the back.
Last year, at a family wedding, my cousin Sherwood
Offered me a shopping cart filled with wine

From his liquor store in New York State
Because of my grandparents' visits, because
My grandmother had made black cows for the kids

And played gin rummy with them on Saturday nights,
Because she had tried to adopt my cousin Larry
After he had been in an institution for years. . . .

We tend to these stories as best we can,
And need to de-code them, and hug them to us
Like our own flawed memories of childhood.

My grandmother died in Skokie Valley Hospital
Eight days before I was married, my grandfather
Never wore the hat he bought for the holidays.

I don't know what is left of them anymore
Except these details rescued from the flames,
These fragments and what we make of them.

2

Wild garlic grew along the banks of the Checagou River
Where Father Pinet established the Mission of the Guardian Angel
Three hundred and forty-four years before my grandfather

Lifted his five-year-old daughter onto his shoulders
And carried her over a filthy body of sludge
That had once flowed eastward towards the lake

With explorers and fur traders, missionaries and settlers.
A resinous drizzle seeped out of the air
And all her life my mother has remembered

Her father pausing in the middle of the Michigan
Avenue Bridge with the city rising around them
On a Sunday night during the Great Depression

And staring down at the polluted depths as if
He were searching for something important, something
The wind rifling the water could tell him,

Its black jaws swallowing the rain like tears
Falling from the pavement, the white shadow
Of the Wrigley Building incandescent in the fog,

The sound of a single foghorn bellowing
At a barge moving vaguely in the distance.
Sitting on her father's shoulders in the rain

Eighteen years before I was born, ninety-seven years
After the Powatomies staged a violent dance
On the shores of a sluggish brown stream

Before their forced migration westward,
My mother saw the stars being extinguished
One by one over the humped bodies of cars

And the girded steel skeletons of skyscrapers
Strung across the Loop like the future itself
And she began to cry. . . .
                              Twenty years later,

After her father had died of a heart attack
In the hospital where my sisters were born,
My mother took us to the double-decked bridge

On Wacker Drive to find a place for her sadness
In the bruised heart of a city of steel and glass,
To begin the piecework of her grief, to stare

Down at the nauseating chowder of fish and garbage
That the Powatomies once called "Garlic Creek."
Black Partridge heard dozens of linden birds

Wailing over the marshy acres and lowlands
Where a black Frenchman founded a trading post
At the mouth of a narrow, curving river

And my mother saw the constellations fading
On a drizzling October night in 1932
In her own small history of grief.

What was her father thinking about in the rain?
His last job as a stringer for a Yiddish newspaper?
His new job selling the *Book of Knowledge*

To people who couldn't afford it? The way
The river had been reversed by a sanitary canal
To avoid polluting the lake? His papa's death?

"Sometimes you have to imagine the past,"
My mother said, and we closed our eyes and smelled
Pungent wild garlic growing along the banks.

3

Some days we need to be given back to ourselves
Like an unexpected present, to be remembered
Not as we are now but as we were

Before the wheel took its turn with us
And the notches began to appear like clockwork
Around our eyes and carved into our foreheads.

That hawkish-looking man slicing roast beef
At a large family gathering was once a boy
Rubbing his eyes and doing homework in the kitchen,

Rolling in the high grass with his puppy, Sarah,
Playing with baseball cards in his room at night
With a tiny flashlight for illumination.

Aunt Gussie thinks that he looks exactly
The way his grandfather looked coming out
Of steerage at Ellis Island seventy-five years ago,

But Uncle Moe believes he has Anna's eyes
And nose, Celia's hands. It's as if these resemblances
Could keep their brother and his wife alive. . . .

But what about those self-begetting men
Who act as if they'd never had relatives,
Those women whose childhoods were so torturous

They remember too much about them—every secret
Insult and hurt, every public humiliation—
And can't escape that vast maternal presence

And chilly paternal absence? Sometimes the past
Is lurking around corners and lying in wait
For us, like a bridge, or the woman

Who introduced herself as the youngest daughter
Of my first father's father's longstanding mistress.
What do you say to a woman in a raffia hat

Who knows a family secret waiting to haunt you?
There are some stories you never wanted to hear
But listened to anyway. And what do you say

To that harried clerk at the Acme Market—
She has four children now—who cracked you
Across the forehead with a wooden broom handle

And sent you screaming home to your grandparents?
That attractive middle-aged woman selling home computers
Was an anorexic teenager you wanted to die for,

And that genteel old man walking his golden retriever
At twilight around the lagoon in the Forest Preserve
Had two sons who committed suicide in college.

It's the way the past, too, is under revision,
Changing as we change, the way our sufferings
Are converted into reasons we can understand.

And there are stories that define us to ourselves
As we go lurching into the future: My grandfather
Is standing on the dock at Ellis Island

While his future wife is wearing a stocking cap
And selling papers on the corner of 95th and Broadway.
There is a skinny girl from Riga on the boat

Who wants to marry him, there is a man
Who tips her ten dollars for the *New York Times*,
But they are already hurtling towards each other,

4

Towards my mother and my aunt, my sisters and me,
Towards that warm autumn night on Coney Island
When the white-capped waves peaked in moonlight

And the red carousel spun madly overhead
In a dappled pattern of shadows and light,
And the shy man with spectacles on his nose

And autumn in his heart—as Isaac Babel said—
Asked the bold woman in a flowering pink dress
With white stockings and matching heels

To marry him, to embrace the blank wave that
Would bring them two daughters and six grandchildren,
One Great Depression and five jobs, a partner

Who cheated them out of thousands of dollars
In the meat business in Rochester, the long train-
Rides back and forth to Chicago, the protests

In Union Square and Grant Park, the laughter
With friends in the back of Moshe Shoshinsky's
Bookstore on Lawrence Avenue, the calm mornings

With the girls lying on Morris Avenue beach,
The years of scrimping by and the sweet pleasure
Of their daughters' weddings in white gowns and hats,

The night that Ida's husband was murdered
Locking up his grocery store in Irving Park,
The winter of mourning that she lived with them,

The trips across the country for the births
Of Roselyn and Sherwood and Larry, the familial
Poloposis that eventually killed Max,

The discussions over sweet rolls and coffee
About the Old World and the New, their first grandchild,
My mother holding me up in the blinding light. . . .

It's like this: Their stories about our childhood
Became our own memories of childhood, their memories
About themselves became our romance of the family,

My grandmother opening a box of dark chocolates
And deciding to fall in love with my grandfather,
My grandfather laughing uncontrollably at the table

About his mother-in-law's maiden name, Zelda Pochapovsky,
Until he was reduced to silence by the silence
Of the women glaring into their plates—

These versions of the truth became our versions
Of how we got here, of how our mothers were
Pulled from the lake and pulled us after them. . . .

I remember the day that my mother took us
To the parking lot across from the hospital
So that we could stand on the hood of the car

And wave to the frail man on the seventh floor
Who was pressing his lips to the window
And waving to us as hard as he could.

I remember how my mother brought the dress
My grandmother would have worn to my wedding
To show her in the hospital. All that's over now.

But tonight when I closed my eyes for a moment
I imagined my unborn daughter and her small son
Pausing in the rain on an empty bridge.

5

I suppose she is telling him how her mother and father
Met at a party in Philadelphia (or was it New York?),
About their first date to a performance of *Hamlet*

At a festival in Central Park, how they clapped
At the slapstick of the guards throwing themselves
On the stage when they heard a ghost calling

And the overdone acting of an overripe Ophelia,
How they walked home on a perfect summer evening
(Her mother would have preferred they take a taxi)

Holding hands and trading quips about their families,
Stopping at a bookstore and a pastry shop
And laughing uproariously at each other's stories,

Their first kiss on the corner of 113th and Broadway. . . .
Her son shifts restlessly on her shoulders,
But my daughter is musing about the first years

Of her parents' marriage, what it meant
When her mother's father died of a heart attack
And her mother's mother developed ovarian cancer,

How they came home from England to care for her
And lived in her mother's childhood bedroom
Surrounded by dolls for an entire year

While her grandmother Gertrude—the one she never
Met and was named after—was dying upstairs.
The next year they moved to Detroit

And her mother seldom went out of the house,
Mourning and practicing nocturnes on the grand piano
Her daughter would inherit, calling herself an orphan.

We are told so much about our parents' lives,
But she can only guess at the years of fertility
Drugs and over-zealous doctors, how it felt

To move to the Southwest for their new jobs,
To take a squalling infant home from an agency
With a social worker in the back seat of the car.

She wonders about the grandfather she saw once
Who was like a character out of *Guys and Dolls*,
A gambler from Odessa transferred to Phoenix,

And the grandmother that she dimly remembers
Smothering her with kisses and waltzing in the room,
Her grandpa Kurt lifting her onto his shoulders.

We pass on what we can of the past—
Which isn't much—a few names and places,
A few recollections around the kitchen table

With the photograph albums that her mother and father
Saved from a fire that destroyed their apartment
One summer in Houston. By now her son Edward

Is beginning to squirm and cry, but she
Pauses for one more moment on the bridge
To imagine her parents daydreaming together,

In honor of their vague yearnings towards
A future that included her, how they managed
To raise her out of the water into a family,

How their lives went on and wore down, intertwined,
How they died and left her in a light rain
With these memories, letters, fragments, stories.

4

Rapture

I felt it on Parents Day in 1963
In a seventh-grade classroom at Fairview School
When my mother stepped into the corner
                                of a winter afternoon,
Her dress stippled in sunlight
                        by the snowy window.

Something about the way
                        she tilted her head
To gaze down at the wire hangers and rubber balls
That I had constructed
                        as a science project
On the motion of planetary bodies

Pierced through me
Like a silver blade glinting
                                in white sunlight,
Or a few haunting notes
                        rising out of a late quartet,
Or the sudden stabbing rage of happiness. . . .

And then I was lost—
The lights in the class dizzied overhead,
A door in the hallway slammed
                                somewhere far off,
And I could hear the voice of a teacher
                        calling to me in the distance,

Though in a moment I was lifted up
                            and transported,
Spinning away from the room
                   in a bright light,
Untethered from earth,
              spiralling into another orbit.

Refusal

I woke up this morning
                thinking about the beefy van-driver
Who used to drag me out of the front-hall closet
While I screamed
            and hung on in desperation
To the rubber boots and plastic raincoats
                  that never saved me.

How pure was that refusal
                in those red mornings of childhood
When I was hauled into the world
Of building blocks and fire trucks
              and bubbles of helium
Rising out of the blue-and-white wallpaper
Towards the false lights
            fastened to the ceiling.

In the dimly-lit back room,
                I can see a row of barred cribs
Lined up against a wall
             papered with constellations.
I can see the bright misshapen moons
                of our parents' faces
Cut out of colorful squares
             and floating over our heads
As if they could protect us from nightmares.

And I can hear the cries of that small boy—
              foundering, lost;
That little Bartleby of the nursery

Moved by a refusal to join
That I remembered this morning
                              as I prepared myself
For the sure unwavering motions of another day.

The Abortion (1969)

I swore I'd always remember
That dingy hotel room in downtown Detroit
Where the doctor came
                  with his gleaming metallic instruments
To carve a newly-forming body
                     out of your body
For 500 dollars in small bills paid in cash.

I swore I'd never forget the exact pressure
Of your hand in mine
                as he prodded open your legs
With a surgical knife
               under a tent of white sheets
While his girlfriend fiddled with the radio
And lounged against the door in her spiked heels.

Afterwards, I remembered three shades of blood
                        staining the bedsheets,
How the doctor sudsed his hands
                  carefully in the sink,
Turning them over twice in the bathroom light.
I remembered the door shutting behind them,
The sound of heels clicking in the hallway
                as an elevator rang in the distance
And I stared into your ashen face. . . .

That night I believed your heavy narcotic sleep
Would never end,
              I cradled your face in my palms
Like a fragile sculpture
And wiped your dampening forehead

                            with a cool washcloth.
It wasn't enough. Nothing helped but rest,
Your body already trying
                  to knit up the emptiness.

I can still feel the relief of that next morning
When you woke up with a surprised moan
                    and a pained smile on your face,
When I saw the fresh light
                crystallizing on your body
As if an angel had sprung back to life.

It's touching to remember us
               in the early morning light,
Two teenagers holding hands on a narrow bed,
A boy and a girl
          not knowing what they've done,
Murderous children lying together in innocence,
An electric joy
        passing back and forth between them. . . .

That was before we told your parents about it,
Before we discovered
         you had never been pregnant,
Before the doctor was arrested
          in a dank hotel room
With a young assistant at his side.

That was before you turned to me years later
In the rain, in a different city,
Almost apologizing
After so much had gone wrong between us,
Saying,
    I'll never forgive you. Nothing is forgiven.

A Photograph Ripped in Half

I don't know what it means
                              to see us in the half-tones
Of a photograph ripped in two,
                              our bodies—
Which had once been joined—split
Into separate black-and-white frames,
The ragged edges of a border
                              that somehow widened
Into an impassable gulf between us.

It's been too long since I've seen you.
I don't know what it means
                              to spend my days walking around
Like a widower
                    with a mourner's Kaddish on his lips
And the mirrors sheeted in his house
In honor of the dead
                    and respect for the living
Who can't stand to see their own reflections.

All day today I thought of your body
Scorched into my memory
                              like a radiant prophecy
That I once believed
                    had already come true—
Wheels and chariots, magnificent war horses
Rising out of the sea's foam,
                              swords flashing,
Golden shields emblazoned by the blinding sun. . . .

I can't bear to remember the light
                              or the dark half-tones
Of our torn photograph, what happened between us,
Your body in sunspots,
                       your body in shadows.
Today, at sunset, the sky hung down
                              like a frayed sheet
About to be split apart by the lightning.
Rain blurred the windows all night long.

Cemeteries by the Sea

for Garrett Hongo

I. HA'IKU

There is a treacherous curve on Route 36
Where the gears grind
                    in your rented metallic body
And the dead are nothing more
                              than a hairpin turn
And a heartbeat away.

                    Above you
A helmet of fire crowns
                    the volcano's ashen head
While the rainbow-colored sails
                              of wind-surfers
Gleam in the white-capped Pacific below.

One day we stopped the car
                    and stumbled
Through a sunshower at dusk:
                              13 wooden crosses
Misted with yellow light,
                    rain borrowed from the ocean,

And a sense of the dead
                    troubling the air
In suits of yellow flame,
                              blowing through the bananas
And the split-leafed palms
                    in spirals of yellow dust.

I believe we had come to lie down
                              in the topsoil,
To remember something essential again,
                                        something we'd lost—
The wild hair of the grass
                      growing in circles and waves,

The eternal, low-pitched voice of the water,

The ancient swimming motions of the dead
                                    touching our faces
As we breathed from the wet air
                            and quietly felt
Our bodies floating out to join them.

2. KAHUKU

It's dawn and the sunlight
Slivers over the cane fields, shaves
Across the scrub grass
                    running down to the Pacific,
Filters through the mangos
                    and the large-veined guavas
Buried under the pretense of darkness.

There are two purple welts on the horizon
And a thimble of yellow dye
                    spilled in the ironwoods
And the fleshy chrysanthemums
                    growing out of the hips
Of the Japanese cemetery by the ocean
Where my friend's ancestors are buried.

We have come here to remove our shoes
In the matted temple grass,
                    to pay our respects
To a few wooden markers washed clean by the rain.
We have come here to see the white birds-of-paradise
Wavering on the cliffside
                    like lamp-lit signals from the sea.

Others have left behind jars of anthuriums
And little plates of food for the dead,
Oranges and rice cakes,
                    glasses of fresh water
To appease the salt-driven thirst
Of those who have disappeared into the ground.
We, too, want to leave signs of our faithfulness.

But we have also come here to find
                              blue clouds of unknowing,
Gutted cars pushed to the side of the road,
Cattle egrets rising languidly
Out of the turquoise waves
                         that have nothing to do
With the brightness of our belief in morning.

I suppose we have come here to wonder
If the dead speak to the living
                          in small gulps of wind,
In a patchwork of fog ascending
                             as the sky tilts
Precariously
          and golden coins materialize in the air.

Cross Portrait

Early winter morning on Fort Street, and the sun
Is an orange heart beating in the smokestacks,
A palette knife scraping the fog from the windows.
At this moment the studio is a mixture of warm colors—
Magentas and pinks, Indian yellows and cadmium reds—
And my friend is stabbing a paintbrush in turpentine.
The glare on his face is steady and unrelenting
Since we've stared at each other for months now

Working on portraits, the huge shapes of his paintings
Expanding around us—compasses and protractors,
Shadows and edges—the sounds from the city
Denting the silence, the trucks grinding in salt
And the trees whistling in their shirtsleeves of ice.
Sometimes the city is a stranger pressing against us—
Unloved, unwanted—a body needing our bodies.
We've stared at each other for too long now

Without understanding. It's the way we've gone on
Talking ourselves away from the silence, evading
The tiny blue lines that are streaking our features,
The gray creases that widen each year on our foreheads,
Blooming around our eyes, forever scarring our faces.
But this morning we held an impossible silence between us
And felt our features finally beginning to weaken
Like masks under a sudden bright intensity of lamps.

It's brutal and moving to stare into another man's face
Hour after hour, to study the stark brilliance of his glare,
To watch the paint slowly accumulating on canvas

Stroke after careful stroke, transforming
A chaos of lines into your own unhappy portrait.
Today, I glimpsed a friend's face mirrored in mine
And watched the sunlight layer our skin with the rawest
Of colors, and felt the spaces dissolving between us.

Infertility

We don't know how to name
                    the long string of zeros
Stretching across winter,
                    the barren places,
The missing birthdates of the unborn.

We'd like to believe in their souls
                    drifting through space
Between the Crab and the Northern Cross,
Smoky and incandescent,
                    longing for incarnation.

We'd like to believe in their spirits descending,
But month after month, year after year,
We have laid ourselves down
                    and raised ourselves up
And not one has ever entered our bodies.

We'd like to believe that we have planted
And tended seeds
                    in their honor,
But the spirits never appear
                    in darkness or light.

We don't know whether to believe in their non-existence
Or their secrecy and evasiveness,
                    their invisible spite.
Maybe it's past us, maybe it's the shape of nothing
Being born,
                    the cold slopes of the absolute.

Proustian

At times it seems lucky and unexpected, the past,
And who we were then, and what the mind brings
Back on an overcast day in late September,

The dense, evanescent clouds shifting overhead,
The wind fingering the branches in the live oaks,
The little chunks of our childhood selves

Floating to the surface after all these years
Like memories that we imagine we imagined,
Or tiny bits of metal constellating on magnets.

One moment we are drinking coffee at the window
On a wet day falling around us, the next moment
We are putting our heads down on our desks

For story-time, or cleaning our lockers,
Or filing into the schoolyard for a fire drill.
Soon we are pulling on sleek yellow slickers

And splashing home in the rain to our parents
And grandparents. I see a boy throwing his arms
Around his grandmother's neck and hugging her.

He eats sugar cookies that he dunks in milk,
And plays in his room by himself now, happily,
In a fort that he has built next to his bed. . . .

Sometimes it is enough just to remember
There was once a time before we knew about time
When the self and the world fit snugly together.

A Note About the Author

Edward Hirsch has published five previous books of poems: *For the Sleepwalkers* (1981), *Wild Gratitude* (1986), which won the National Book Critics Circle Award, *The Night Parade* (1989), *Earthly Measures* (1994), and *On Love* (1998). He has also written three prose books, including *How to Read a Poem and Fall in Love with Poetry* (1999), a national best-seller, and *The Demon and the Angel: Searching for the Source of Artistic Inspiration* (2002). A frequent contributor to leading magazines and periodicals, including *The New Yorker, DoubleTake,* and *The American Poetry Review,* he also writes the Poet's Choice column for the *Washington Post Book World.* He has received the Prix de Rome, a Guggenheim Fellowship, an American Academy of Arts and Letters Award for Literature, and a MacArthur Fellowship. A professor in the Creative Writing Program at the University of Houston for seventeen years, he is now President of the John Simon Guggenheim Memorial Foundation.

A Note on the Type

This book was set on the Linotype in Granjon, a type named in compliment to Robert Granjon, type cutter and printer in Antwerp, Lyons, Rome, Paris. Granjon, the boldest and most original designer of his time, was one of the first to practice the trade of type founder apart from that of printer.

Linotype Granjon was designed by George W. Jones, who based his drawings on a face used by Claude Garamond (1510–1561) in his beautiful French books. Granjon more closely resembles Garamond's own type than do any of the various modern faces that bear his name.

Composed by Heritage Printers,
Charlotte, North Carolina
Printed and bound by United Book Press,
Baltimore, Maryland
Designed by Harry Ford